beyond
your
number

an enneagram journal
to guide you forward
with greater wholeness

Type 9

Stephanie J Spencer

Certified Enneagram Coach

stephaniejspencer.com

with special thanks to

Ashley M Leusink
for graphic design and layout support
find out about her work as a spiritual director at
jesusandgin.com

Rachel McCauley
for copyediting support
find out about her work at
linkedin.com/in/rachel-d-mccauley

this journal is dedicated to

my family
who supports me, laughs with me, loves me,
and has been patient with me in the messy process
of finding my way as an enneagram coach.

my friends
who nerd out with me in enneagram conversations,
help me stay grounded and connected,
and remind me of the power of human belonging.

my clients
who teach me what it is to live as their enneagram types,
and give me wisdom to pass along
to others in my work.

Dear Reader,

Enneagram is not a personality test. It is a tool that gives insight into who we are and why we do what we do. These insights are intended to help us move forward in wholeness, freeing us from the passions and fixations of our types.

But knowing how to break out of these confines can prove difficult. We read books, listen to podcasts, follow Instagram accounts, and are left with the question, "Now what?"

The work can be daunting. This journal is meant to guide you through the forward movement of enneagram.

Its questions are designed to open space for you to see your behaviors, motivations, fears, and hopes with more clarity and compassion. The more honest we are with ourselves, the more insight we have into what practices might help us move forward in wholeness.

Growth is more like a wide and rocky river to navigate than a narrow set of steps to climb. Two people who are the same enneagram type may need to focus on vastly different areas of change. Our paths toward greater wholeness will be as diverse and unique as our backgrounds. Therefore, this journal is meant to be worked through as a winding path, taking you where you believe you need to go. It is not a fixed path from Point A to Point B.

The place where one person begins could be an ending place for another. The work you have already done might be the work someone else needs to begin.

I hope you will look through this journal, and allow questions to "rise from the page." The question that sticks out to you now is the one to sit with today. Answer it. Let a new question rise off the page when you are ready. Go at your own pace. Stay with a question as long as necessary: a day, a week, or a month. There isn't a right or a wrong pace.

However you engage with this journal, I hope it helps you on your journey of becoming the best version of you.

In hope,
Stephanie

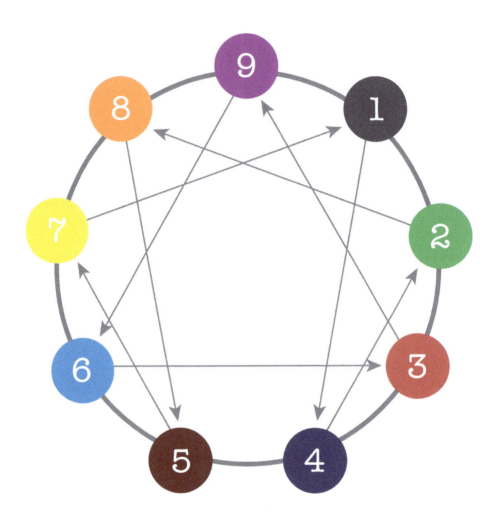

an enneagram overview

Enneagram is a framework that gives us insight into nine primary ways people engage in the human experience. These nine numbers are the enneagram types. The symbol that holds these numbers is a visual picture of the energy and interaction of the types. It is a framework that holds both complexity and unity, allowing us to be both a lot like other people and uniquely ourselves.

The circle reminds us we are all connected. We hold and display all numbers to some extent. However, we rest in one number as our home-base.

Our home-base enneagram type is the lens through which we see and experience the world.

When we know our type, we find language for the underlying factors that motivate us. We think about things like what we are afraid of, what we desire, and what makes us feel vulnerable. Knowing our enneagram number helps us name our shadows with compassion and take steps to live more deeply into our gifts.

No enneagram type is better or worse than another type. This is why numbers are more helpful than titles. As soon as we add words, there are things we do and don't want to be.

All nine enneagram types carry important facets of what it means to be human.

Each type is more of a spectrum than a point. We draw on the numbers next to our type as well, often drawing on one more strongly than the other. These adjacent numbers are called our wings.

Numbers connected to us by lines reflect our movement toward other types. In stressful states, we move with the arrow, compelled toward behaving like that type. In relaxed or secure states, we move against the arrow, opening to receiving the energy of the other type moving toward us.

Our enneagram number and its connected points are all important parts of who we are. We need to learn how to move in and receive the energies of each of them in order to move forward in wholeness.

recommended resources

This guided journal is meant to be a resource for those who already know their enneagram type and are familiar with the system. If enneagram is new to you, or you want to learn more, here are some places to explore.

websites

integrative9.com

enneagraminstitute.com

drdaviddaniels.com

podcasts

The 27 Subtypes of the Enneagram by The Liturgists

Typology with Ian Morgan Cron

The Enneagram Journey by Suzanne Stabile

music

Atlas: Enneagram by Sleeping at Last

primers

Enneagram Spectrum of Personality Styles by Jerome Wagner

The Road Back to You by Ian Morgan Cron and Suzanne Stabile

Enneagram Magazine Issue #1

deeper dives

The Complete Enneagram by Beatrice Chestnut

The Enneagram in Love and Work by Helen Palmer

The Sacred Enneagram by Chris Heuertz

The Wisdom of the Enneagram by Don Riso and Russ Hudson

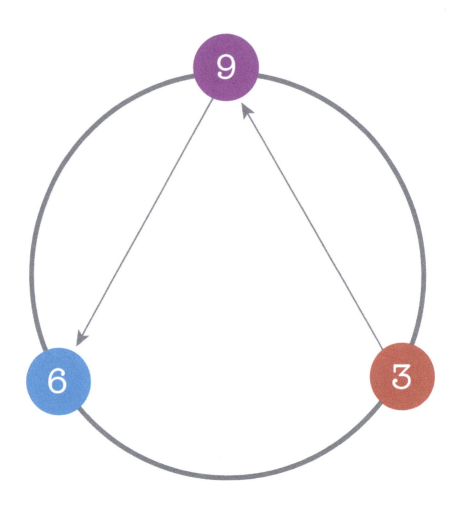

an overview of Type 9

Enneagram Type 9s desire harmony. They are easygoing and mediating, as they see the world from multiple perspectives. They want to go with the flow, and provide a supportive presence to those around them. However, their hope for harmony can turn Type 9s conflict-avoiding instead of peace-making, as they substitute comfort for understanding. They can become complacent and passive, settling for what they get. Their fear of separation and tendency toward resignation combine and cause Type 9s to merge with others and lose their own identity.

As they find their voice and strength of being, Type 9s display the virtue of engagement, which allows them to connect and love instead of just merge and settle. This helps them experience collaboration, belonging, and purpose.

When Type 9s feel stress, they connect with the energy of Type 6, which can look like increased worry, indecisiveness, or responsibility.

When Type 9s feel secure, they connect with the energy of Type 3, which can access traits of productivity, image-management, or strategic leadership.

why purple?

Purple combines the stability of blue (Type 6) and the energy of red (Type 3). It retains both warm and cool properties, and is thought to represent wisdom and creativity, and spirituality.

Purple is the color of lavender, a flower that is both calming and healing. It is thought to be the color of spiritual awakening that shows someone is being guided by their mind and led by their heart, the hope for a healthy Type 9.

At the same time, too much purple is thought to create irritability, something that can be a struggle for 9s if they feel backed into a corner.

Type 9s are part of the Receptive or Withdrawing triad, along with Types 4s (indigo) and Type 5s (cognac). These three colors have an inward-facing energy. They are open and receptive when more healthy, and struggle with inertia and connection when less healthy.

When Type 9s feel secure, they access the bright red of Type 3, perhaps taking on a tone that is more plum. They are still calm, but with more forwardness and flavor.

Stop acting so small.
You are the universe in
ecstatic motion.

Rumi

Enneagram is a map and a guide.
It does not describe the entire geography of the human landscape. It is meant to help us grow in awareness and move towards health and wholeness. It is not intended to hold every nuance and attribute of a human person.
I am an enneagram type.
I am ALSO a unique individual.

In what ways does enneagram Type 9 describe me?

In what ways does enneagram Type 9 not describe me?

How can I keep the tensions between my uniqueness and enneagram Type 9 in mind as I do this work?

Are there any potential barriers keeping me from
doing the work of the enneagram?

Can I remove some of these barriers
before diving deeper?

What resources do I need in order to engage in the work of the enneagram? (i.e. intentional time)

Are there concrete supports that would help me move forward? (i.e. a friend with whom to process)

What is making me feel vulnerable, defensive, or afraid right now?

Do any of these things need to be resolved before moving forward with this journal?

Can I look at my habits with compassion
and choose to change them to reflect the values
true to my essence?

What might keep me from seeing myself with hope,
possessing the potential for change?

Can I use the enneagram as a tool to become more embodied and present to my life and relationships?

Can I keep this posture and goal in mind as I keep moving forward?

Are there ways I am trapped within
my enneagram type?

How do I need to recognize the transformation I have
already done before beginning the work of this
journal?

words that can be used to describe Type 9

patient   easygoing   mediating

conflict-avoiding   neutral   agreeable

self-effacing   comfort-seeking   settled

stubborn   reassuring   calm

tedious   modest   passive-aggressive

peaceful   grounded   harmonious

unself-conscious   indolent   narcoticizing

neglectful   diplomatic   permissive

non-judgmental   flexible   unflappable

supportive   distracted   low energy

What are three words I like?

What are three words I don't like?

What are three words that once
described me but no longer do?

What are three words that describe me now?

Talk to yourself like you
would to someone you love.

Brené Brown

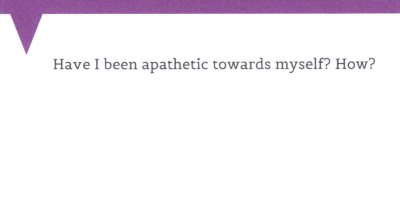

on inertia

Have I been apathetic towards myself? How?

What would open me to putting more energy into my life?

When have I taken the resigned stance that it's not worth it to try?

Has this held me back from relationships or dreams?

When have I been overly passive, waiting
for things to take their course?

What might have happened if I stepped forward
in action sooner?

Does my ability to see and feel all sides of things keeping me from being able to prioritize tasks and schedule?

Where am I frozen? Why?

How have I been able to recognize the needs of others and support them well?

How can I celebrate this contribution?

Have habits and busywork been ways of delaying action I am afraid to take?

Can I see the difference between merging and companioning with someone?

In what relationships have I lost myself?

How has my easy-going presence offered
support to others?

How has stubbornness affected my relationships?

When has my slowness to make decisions caused
pain or frustration to those around me?

When has it helped those around me?

How has my easy-going presence offered
support to others?

When is the last time I said no?
Have I let unmet desires simmer into resentment?

on presence

How would it feel to bring a stronger, more confident, and more boundaried presence into the world?

Would it change my life, work, and relationships? How?

Do I let my own preferences slip away in service to the peaceful environment I seek?

What is the difference between a harmony that does not include my preferences and a peace I have negotiated with my own needs in mind?

Am I able to sense the internal states of others?

How has that helped me come alongside them?

When I am around people, do I absorb their energy? When is this helpful? When is this not helpful?

How is the energy I get from others different from the energy I receive when I am by myself?

Tell me, what is it you plan
to do with your one wild
and precious life?

Mary Oliver

on comfort

What do I need? What do I prefer?
Have I confused needs with inessentials?

How has this affected my trajectory?

Are there ways I numb and comfort myself through pleasure and relaxation?

What habits have I developed in order to avoid discomfort or stress?

How has my desire for comfort in the present
held me back from choices that could improve my future?

What would help me risk frustration or disquiet
more often?

When have I experienced a hardship that was worth it, either for the good in my own life or in the world?

How could I hold these experiences in mind when I face decisions that could cause unease?

How have I defaulted to passive aggressive behavior/communication instead of direct and clear conflict?

What if I changed this pattern?

Do I avoid conflicts?

How am I holding the feelings of this tension?

What would happen if I moved toward conflicts?

When have I expressed my ability to be a peacemaker who can hold multiple perspectives?

How do confrontation and disrespect make me feel vulnerable? How has this affected my choices?

When have I held back my opinion out of fear
that it would cause tension?

How might my relationships be better if there were room
for multiple opinions?

How do I see peace and harmony valued and reflected in my life?

How have I fallen asleep to myself?

What would it take to wake up?

They had carried the truth of themselves in a sheltered place inside the flesh, exactly the way a fruit that has gone soft still carries inside itself the clean, hard stone of its future.

Barbara Kingsolver

Our first response to stress tends to be
to "double down" in our primary type.

In higher levels of stress, Type 9 moves toward Type 6.
The movement can be unhealthy or healthy,
paralyzing or resourcing.

Words that might describe a Type 6 include
cooperative, rigid, tenacious, responsible, vigilant, skeptical,
cautious, prepared, loyal, dogmatic, worried, insightful, respectful,
defensive, practical, rule-challenger, rule-follower

When I feel stress, do I get stubborn, avoid difficulty, seek comfort
or display other stereotypical traits of Type 9?

Are there times when stress has made me feel like
a "different person"?

In stress, am I slipping into the less healthy
characteristics of Type 6 and

... becoming more structured in order to find
security or comfort?

... turning fearful or ruminative about all that could happen?

... moving away from forward movement by looking outside
of myself for approval or guidance?

In stress, am I connecting with the healthier characteristics of a Type 6 and

... finding a loyalty towards myself and others that has empowered me to act?

... discovering the courage to step forward with my opinions and positions?

... giving to and supporting others instead of merging with them?

Integrating my inner Type 6 will help me move forward in wholeness.

Can I consciously open myself to the healthier characteristics of this type?

When I feel secure, I may feel or act differently than I do at other times, and even from the typical descriptions of my enneagram type.

In security, Type 9 moves toward Type 3.
The movement can be unhealthy or healthy, paralyzing or resourcing.

Words that might describe a Type 3 include productive, successful, competent, busy, pragmatic, ambitious, image-conscious, successful, performing, workaholic, trendy, arrogant, outgoing, scheming, popular, recognition-seeking

Some people might feel secure on a day off, or on vacation, or at home, or with a trusted friend.

What helps me feel secure?

In security, am I slipping into the less healthy characteristics of a Type 3 and

... engaging in busywork as a distraction from what I really need to be doing?

... falling into playing a role that distances me even more from my true self?

... looking to achievement to give me love or purpose?

In security, when am I connecting with the healthier characteristics of a Type 3 and

... feeling my worth and ability to be successful?

... setting goals, working towards them, and finishing what I've begun?

... connecting to my preferences and finding the energy to move towards what I want?

Integrating my inner Type 3 will help me move forward with wholeness.

Can I consciously open myself to the healthier characteristics of this type?

If you could only sense how important you are to the lives of those you meet; how important you can be to the people you may never even dream of. There is something of yourself that you leave at every meeting with another person.

Fred Rogers

How have I cultivated my presence to be attentive
to experiences with the posture of yes?

Are others experiencing the virtue of
engagement emanating from my heart?

How are my actions making the world more harmonious?

How am I expressing my gift of being open and
accepting to others?

Am I offering sustainable action and supportive
presence to those around me?

How have I gained a strength of presence that enables me to accept others while bringing my voice and desires into the conversation?

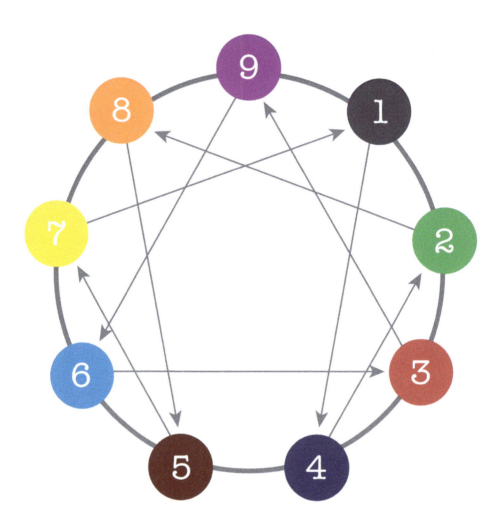

now what?

The question at the beginning of this journal re-surfaces. You have read books, listened to podcasts, perused websites, and followed Instagram accounts. Additionally, you have worked through this journal. I hope what you've written here will continue to be a reference that leads you to better, more complete versions of yourself.

But the question remains... now what?

Keep moving forward. It takes continual work to stay aware of ourselves. This world has a tendency to lull us to sleep.

Actively keep the characteristics, habits, and passions of your Type in your mind as you move through daily choices. Celebrate ways you have grown and notice where you still have room to move forward.

Take time to learn about numbers other than your own. Notice ways other Types exist in some way within you. If there is work to do there, open yourself up to it. (This may be especially useful with your stress response and security numbers.)

Ask the people in your life about their Types, and notice the similarities and differences in how you experience the world. Use enneagram as a tool to help you grow in compassion towards others.

Breathe. Be. Stay in touch with your body. Ground your questions with presence.

You may want to keep this journal to look at once or twice a year. Notice how your answers change. Celebrate the journey.

And if you get discouraged, maybe you can take with you one of my favorite quotes, from Parker Palmer,

"What a long time it can take to become the person you've always been."

From one becomer to another,
Stephanie

CPSIA information can be obtained
at www.ICGtesting.com
Printed in the USA
JSHW012041200520
5806JS00003B/17